Cambridge **Discovery Education**™

▶ **INTERACTIVE READERS**

Series editor: Bob Hastings

SKIN

B2

Caroline Shackleton and Nathan Paul Turner

CAMBRIDGE
UNIVERSITY PRESS

Discovery
EDUCATION™

CAMBRIDGE UNIVERSITY PRESS
Cambridge, New York, Melbourne, Madrid, Cape Town,
Singapore, São Paulo, Delhi, Mexico City

Cambridge University Press
32 Avenue of the Americas, New York, NY 10013-2473, USA

www.cambridge.org
Information on this title: www.cambridge.org/9781107641891

First published 2014

Printed in Hong Kong, China, by Golden Cup Printing Company Limited

A catalog record for this publication is available from the British Library.

Library of Congress Cataloging-in-Publication Data

Shackleton, Caroline.
  Skin / Caroline Shackleton and Nathan Paul Turner.
     pages cm. -- (Cambridge discovery interactive readers)
  ISBN 978-1-107-64189-1 (pbk. : alk. paper)
  1. Skin--Juvenile literature. 2. English language--Textbooks for foreign speakers. 3. Readers
(Elementary) I. Title.

QP88.5.S44 2013
612.7'9--dc23

                                      2013024142

ISBN 978-1-107-64189-1

Additional resources for this publication at www.cambridge.org

Layout services, art direction, book design, and photo research: Q2ABillSMITH GROUP
Editorial services: Hyphen S.A.
Audio production: CityVox, New York
Video production: Q2ABillSMITH GROUP.

Contents

Before You Read: Get Ready! 4

CHAPTER 1
Skin 6

CHAPTER 2
The First Line of Defense 8

CHAPTER 3
Body Art 12

CHAPTER 4
Makeup 18

CHAPTER 5
Protecting Your Skin 22

CHAPTER 6
What Do You Think? 24

After You Read 26

Answer Key 28

Glossary

Before You Read:
Get Ready!

Skin plays an essential part in the daily lives of humans and animals, from protecting and hiding us, to helping us stand out from the crowd.

Words to Know

Complete the definitions with the correct words.

acne   cosmetics   lipstick

suntan   tattoo   wrinkles

❶ _____ : small folds in the skin

❷ _____ : permanent drawing or writing made by putting ink under the skin

❸ _____ : creams, oils, or makeup to put on the face or body that are intended to improve its appearance or quality

❹ _____ : a makeup for coloring a person's lips

❺ _____ : a skin problem, common in young people

❻ _____ : a darker skin color that comes from being in the sun

Words to Know

Read the paragraph. Then complete the definitions with the correct highlighted words.

The word *camouflage* first began to be used in English at the beginning of the 20th century. It is used to describe the painting of vehicles or using different colored dyes on soldiers' uniforms to make them harder to see. In nature, many animals take advantage of this, both predators on the hunt and prey trying to escape with their lives. While humans use clothes to camouflage themselves, animals often use one of their body's organs, their skin.

❶ _____ : a chemical used to change the color of something

❷ _____ : a creature that is hunted and killed for food by another animal

❸ _____ : a part of the body that performs a special job, like the heart or brain

❹ _____ : a design that makes someone or something hard to see in a particular environment

❺ _____ : an animal that hunts and kills other animals for food

? PREDICT

What do you think is the most important function of skin for humans and animals?

CHAPTER 1

Skin

THE ORGAN THAT'S ALWAYS ON DISPLAY.

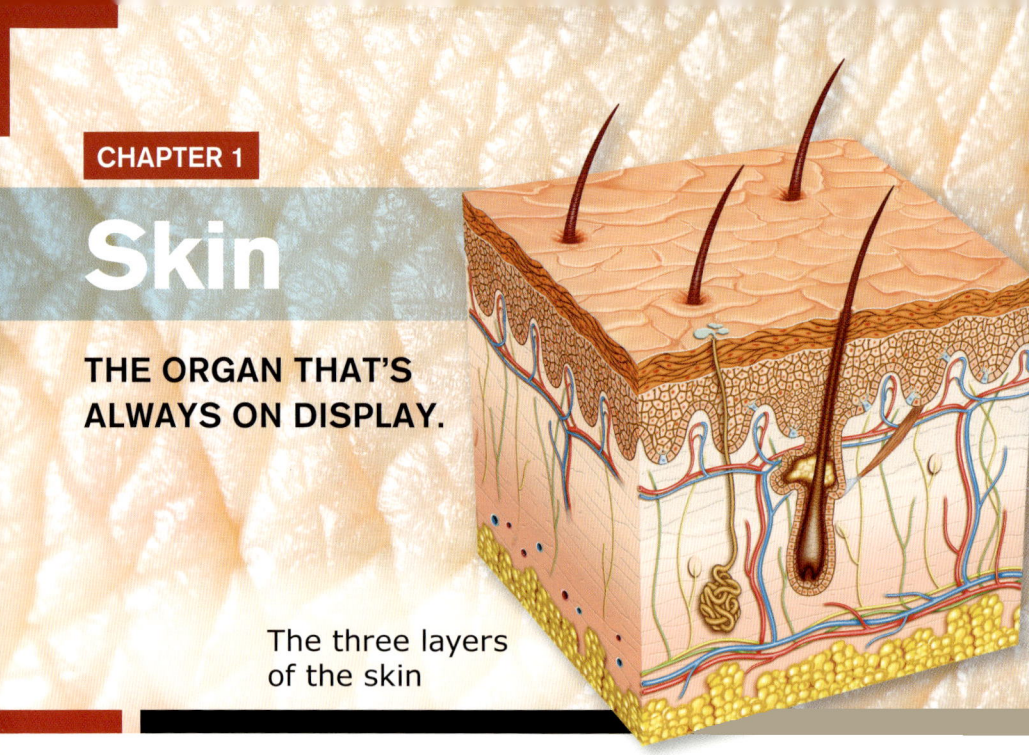

The three layers
of the skin

When we think of our body's organs, words like heart, brain, or stomach come to mind. However, there is one we often forget about – our skin. Skin is so important that it even forms part of our personal identity. Our skin's color, created by a chemical in the body called melanin, is one of the first things other people notice about us. The amount of melanin in our skin depends on our genes, though it can be increased through contact with sunlight.

Skin is made up of three layers: the epidermis, the dermis, and the subcutis. The epidermis, the outer layer, includes dead skin cells that are constantly falling away and being replaced. It is a defensive layer that protects us from the sun, wind, and water.

Below the epidermis lies the dermis. This layer has small organs called **sweat** glands. These help control our body's temperature by sending a water-rich liquid – sweat – up to the epidermis. When this sweat reaches the skin, it has a cooling effect on the body.

In the dermis are also millions of tiny nerve endings. These let us feel and judge everything we come into contact with, from a breath of wind to the temperature of water.

The nerve endings in the dermis are found at different depths and react to the movement of body hair, pressure,[1] vibration,[2] and temperature. These nerve endings let us react quickly to our environment and avoid objects that might hurt us. Our sense of touch is possibly the

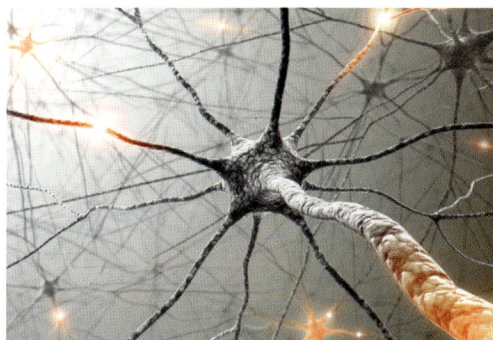

The skin is full of nerve endings, making it very sensitive.

most noticeable of the skin's characteristics because the feelings of pleasure or pain it provides are so powerful.

Below the dermis lies the subcutis. It is made up of many fat cells that help the body hold in heat. These cells also help soften the stresses placed on the body. This layer also contains the roots of our hair.

[1] **pressure:** the force produced by pressing against something
[2] **vibration:** move quickly backward and forward

A rhinoceros

CHAPTER 2

The First Line of Defense

THE SKIN PLAYS A KEY ROLE IN THE FIGHT TO STAY ALIVE.

Human skin can vary from as thick as 1.5 millimeters on the hands and feet to as thin as 0.05 millimeters around the eyes, which is why this is often the first place to show signs of aging. However, some animals, the rhinoceros for example, have skin that can be four centimeters thick!

Skin, however, is more than just physical armor.[3] It can also camouflage an animal from hunters, predators, or prey. This effect makes it possible for an animal to almost disappear into the background.

Perhaps the best example of the power of camouflage is the chameleon. This lizard is so good at changing its appearance that we use the word chameleon to describe people who change depending on the situation.

[3] **armor:** strong protective covering, especially for the body

However, only a few **species** of chameleon change color to camouflage themselves. One of them is the Smith's dwarf chameleon, which can seem almost invisible when not moving. Although many species of chameleons can change color, most do so not to hide, but because of changes in their emotional state or body temperature.

The Namaqua Chameleon lives in the desert. It changes color to protect itself from the extreme temperatures. In the cool morning it turns dark to absorb, or take in, heat more efficiently. In the hot sun it turns a light gray to reflect, or keep out, the sun's heat.

Some animals take advantage of color changes to protect themselves from predators over a longer period of time. Arctic foxes have two different coats, one for summer and one for winter. The winter coat is white to hide the fox in the snow. The fox loses this fur in spring and replaces it with a gray coat more suited to the gray rocks of the arctic summer. Interestingly, the arctic hare, a common prey of the fox, takes advantage of exactly the same color changes!

A chameleon   An arctic fox

A polar bear   A leopard

Other animals have permanent camouflage. A polar bear's white fur makes it almost disappear against the snow and ice, despite its huge size. Strangely enough, the skin below the polar bear's fur is black!

Although the **patterns** on the fur of tigers and leopards are very different, both serve the same purpose – to make it harder for their prey to see them. The patterns are different because they live in different places.

[4] **rodent:** a small animal such as a mouse or a rat with large, sharp front teeth

Video Quest

Porcupines

Watch this video about the North American porcupine. How does this large rodent,[4] the porcupine, defend itself?

Leopards hunt in bush country. Their spots allow them to disappear into the surrounding bushes. Tigers live in the jungle. Their stripes help them hide in the light and shade from the trees and long grass. These stripes are so effective that "tiger stripe" camouflage is used by many armies as a jungle uniform.

Sometimes, however, an animal's skin color seems like a strange choice, almost a mistake. Take the zebra, which seems to draw attention to itself with its striking black and white pattern. Although scientists don't yet know the exact reason for the pattern, one **theory** is that when many zebras run together in a group, they make a pattern which is visually[5] confusing. This makes it difficult for predators, such as lions, to identify one zebra to attack.

This idea was copied in the First World War when British boats were painted in many different patterns to confuse the enemy. However, the technique, known as dazzle camouflage, was never proven to work. Another theory suggests that zebra stripes are actually very effective in hiding the animal in long grass because lions are in fact colorblind!

....

[5] **visually:** relating to seeing or appearance

CHAPTER 3

Body Art

PEOPLE HAVE ALWAYS USED THEIR OWN SKIN TO MAKE A PERMANENT STATEMENT ABOUT WHO THEY ARE.

In 1991 a couple walking in the mountains of northern Italy came across the frozen body of a dead man. When the ice was removed, it was realized that the body was, in fact, a 5,000-year-old mummy, one of the oldest of its kind ever found.

The almost perfectly preserved mummy, named Ötzi after the Ötztal Alps where he was found, was dressed in clothes made of grass and animal skin and carried well-made tools. One of the most striking things, however, was a series of more than 50 tattooed lines and crosses down the man's back, on his legs, and around his ankles and wrists. The marks may have been used as acupuncture. In any case, they obviously had some meaning for Ötzi, and they certainly show that, in the society in which he lived, the art of body decoration existed.

Body decoration for both men and women has been important for many **tribes** and cultures around the world and goes back to the earliest human civilizations. As well as Ötzi, 2,000-year-old mummies with tattoos have been found in both Egypt and parts of Asia.

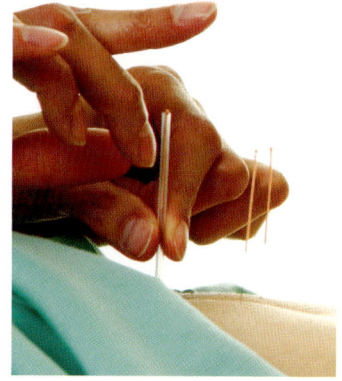

Acupuncture is used in medicine.

In Europe, many tribes traditionally tattooed themselves. It is possible that the word *Britain* comes from an old British word meaning "people of the designs," possibly from their war paint or tattoos. The Romans and Japanese both used tattoos to mark criminals. In the 10th century, an Arab diplomat described meeting Scandinavians "tattooed from their fingernails

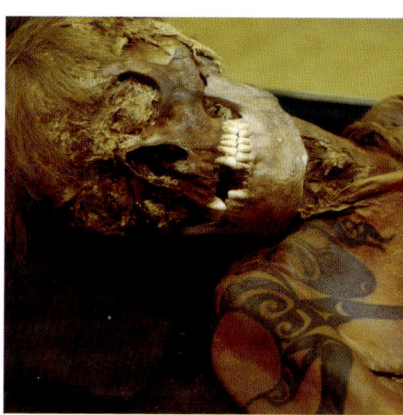

A tattooed mummy

to neck." Several stories tell how, after the battle of Hastings in Britain, the dead body of the last Saxon king of England, Harold Godwinson, could only be identified from his tattoos.

Early Christians, however, connected many of these traditions with old pagan[6] ways, and so eventually, tattooing became a forgotten art in the Western world.

[6] **pagan:** about a religion in which people pray to many gods

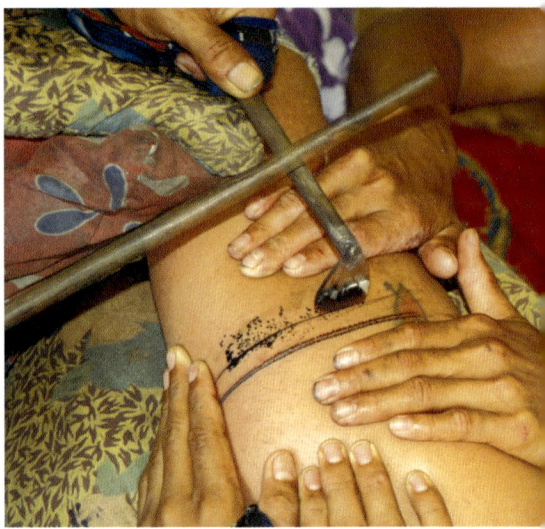

Tattooing is a form of scarification – the practice of making cuts on the body in a particular pattern that remain as permanent **scars** after the cuts **heal**. Scarification is a way to show social or political status.[7] In scarification, a material like mud is often added to the cut to create a bigger or colored scar. Such scars eventually led to the development of tattoos.

The word *tattoo* was first introduced into English from Samoan. In 1769, Captain James Cook came into contact with tattooed Samoan islanders. The original Samoan word *tatau*, means "to strike," referring to hitting the skin with special bone tools to make tiny cuts. These cuts were then filled with an ink made from a burned fruit. The traditional tatau covers the legs and waist of Samoan men. It is extremely painful to be tattooed and is seen as a test of a man's courage.

....

[7] **status:** position, especially in a social group

After seeing the Samoan tattoos, and later the tattooed *moko* face designs of the New Zealand Maoris, some of Captain Cook's crew let themselves be tattooed. This started a tradition among sailors. By the mid-1800s, tattooing had become highly popular and led to the setting-up of tattoo shops by sailors in ports all over the world.

However, it wasn't just sailors who were fascinated by this art form. A tattooed Polynesian islander called Omai, who traveled to Britain with Cook, caused great excitement among the nobility.[8] In the 19th century, tattoos became more acceptable among the upper classes of British society. By the late 19th century, the fashion had caught on in the Royal Family, and both Edward VII of England and his son George V got tattoos, starting a royal tradition.

Most people, however, found this unusual new art strange or disturbing. In most of Western society, tattoos became associated with alternative social groups.

[8] **nobility:** the class or group of people who have a high social position, especially from birth

ANALYZE

How do traditions (or practices), such as body art, spread from culture to culture?

More recently, thanks to movies and pop culture, tattooing has enjoyed a huge growth in popularity. Tattoo art is one of the fastest growing industries in the USA: one in 10 people now has a tattoo.

Many people remain suspicious of tattoos, and while tattooed pop stars are acceptable, tattooed bank managers are not. A recent study showed that people with tattoos were seen as less responsible and trustworthy. But the same study found that tattoos had no effect at all on how attractive a person was considered to be.

Mixed opinions about tattoos can also be found in other cultures. In Japan, tattooing was an important part of tribal culture, but after the introduction of Chinese culture and Buddhism in the 6th century, it began to lose popularity.

Later, in the 17th to 19th centuries, the success of a romantic novel with tattooed heroes made the art hugely popular again. But at that time, tattooing was also used to mark criminals, and so it was often viewed negatively.

Finally, in the 19th century, tattooing was banned, forcing many tattooed people to the edges of society and into criminal groups. Consequently, tattooing became a mark of identity for many criminal groups.

At the beginning of the 21st century, however, the fashion for tattoos is stronger than ever all over the world. They are seen as art and a form of self-expression. Tattoos can still be controversial,[9] though, and are still probably not the best thing to show off at work!

....
[9] **controversial:** causing or likely to cause disagreement

Video Quest

The Tattoo Artist

Watch this video to learn about a tattoo artist in Japan. In the past, who were the only people permitted to have tattoos? Why?

CHAPTER 4

Makeup

GIVING MOTHER NATURE A HELPING HAND.

Originally from the Greek *kosmos*, or "order," *cosmetics* was the word for the art of arranging hair, face, and dress. Today this word usually refers to makeup.

Traditionally, many tribes have used makeup in both religious ceremonies and wars. The signs and marks people painted on their faces and bodies were designed to give them magical powers or to terrify their enemies. Nowadays, some people still refer to makeup as "war paint."

Around 4,000 years ago, Ancient Egyptian women painted their lips and eyes to make them seem bigger. Cleopatra is known to have colored her lips deep red with a dye made from insects. In the 10th century CE, an Arabian doctor called Abulcasis invented lipstick.

The stick, a colored bar of pressed oils, wasn't seen much in Europe, as the Catholic Church quickly banned any sort of lip paint as immoral![10]

In many ancient societies, a suntan was seen as a sign of low social status, the result of having to do hard work in the fields. Upper-class women in both ancient Greece and Rome tried very hard to make their skin as

pale as possible, using a thick makeup made from chalk, animal fat, and often even from lead. Lead is an extremely poisonous metal. Throughout history people have died from using it to lighten their skin.

Chalk

Despite the dangers, pale skin continued to be popular throughout the Middle Ages and beyond. One famous example was Elizabeth I of England, whose thick white mask of makeup helped give her an emotionless, royal expression. Even Victorian women, who considered makeup like lipstick to be immoral, applied mixtures to lighten their faces. Some even went as far as eating chalk in the mistaken belief that it would make them pale!

Queen Elizabeth's white makeup looked like a mask to some people.

[10] **immoral:** not behaving in a way most people consider to be correct

By the beginning of the 20th century, the fashion for pale skin had started to change. First, it was much less common for people in modern society to work in the fields. Also, doctors were beginning to realize how important the sun was for good health. In the 1920s, the famous fashion designer Coco Chanel made darker skin fashionable after she got a suntan while on a boating trip.

By that time, advances in theater makeup were giving movie actresses a much more realistic color and

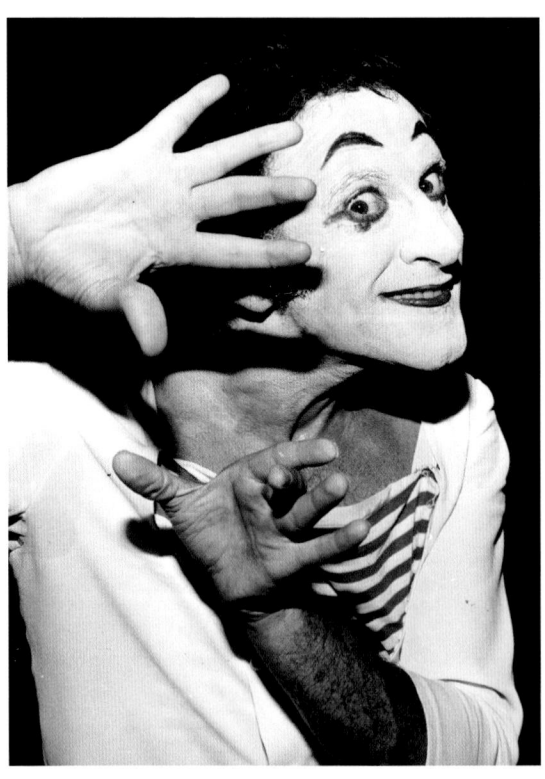

seemingly perfect and healthy skin. Stage makeup had originally been thick and heavy to make actors' expressions stand out from a distance. It was made with animal fat, and was so rough that when it was taken off, it often took skin with it!

The invention of the film camera allowed audiences to see actors' faces close up, allowing makeup to become thinner and softer. Perhaps that's why the rise of the film star made makeup more popular. Millions of women wanted to look like the beautiful Hollywood stars they went to see every Saturday at the movies.

Suddenly, cosmetics companies like Max Factor, which had previously only made cosmetics for actors, found there was a huge demand for makeup among the general public.

Today, makeup is still closely connected with the glamour of Hollywood. Now, as much as ever, cosmetics companies rely on the attraction of Hollywood stars to sell their makeup.

? EVALUATE

What has had a bigger influence on women's opinions about makeup: health or Hollywood? Why do you think so?

CHAPTER 5

Protecting Your Skin

YOUR SKIN PROTECTS YOU, BUT DO YOU PROTECT YOUR SKIN?

Today, we are more aware of the need to protect our skin. Let's look at some dangers to our skin and how to avoid them to keep skin as healthy and attractive as possible.

Keep out of the sun

Although a healthy suntan is attractive, too much sun causes wrinkles and puts us at risk of skin cancer. Although sun is a natural source of vitamin D, scientists think that 15–20 minutes of sun on our skin every day is enough to get healthy amounts of this essential vitamin. Don't overdo it. Wear protective sunblock and clothing if you plan to be outside for a long time.

Keep your skin clean

Clean skin is important. Don't touch **pimples** or wash them too much. Touching and washing too much will irritate the area even more. One of the best ways to clean your skin when you have pimples is by using a steam[11] bath.

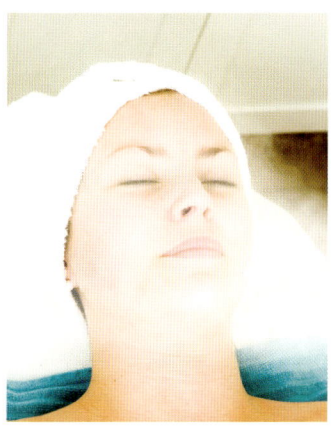

Moisturize

Your skin is continually losing moisture.[12] It gets dried out by the sun, wind, pollution, makeup, and even washing! The resulting dry skin gets easily damaged and ages quickly. It is a good idea to moisturize your skin using a good cream or oil. There are many natural oils that can be used to keep your skin healthy and looking fresh.

Look after your insides

Your skin is a mirror of your general level of health. Stress, lack of sleep, and bad diet will all make your skin worse. Don't smoke. Apart from the risk of cancer, the chemical stresses that smoking puts on your body are one of the biggest causes of old-looking skin. Try to eat healthful foods, exercise, and relax!

[11] **steam:** the hot gas that is produced when water boils
[12] **moisture:** very small drops of water, either in the air or on a surface

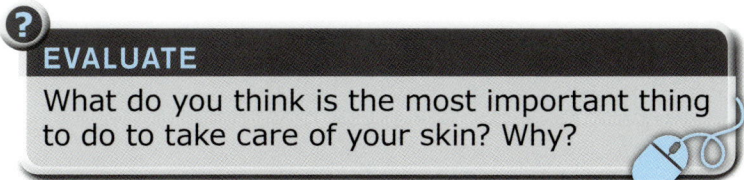

EVALUATE
What do you think is the most important thing to do to take care of your skin? Why?

CHAPTER 6

What Do You Think?

WHAT IS THE PRICE OF BEAUTY?

Makeup is a multi-billion dollar business. In the United States alone, the cosmetics industry creates roughly 10 billion dollars of business a year. Yet the industry has many critics,[13] including defenders of animal rights. Studies show that 95 percent of all animal testing is done to test cosmetics. But many people believe this is a cruel and unnecessary activity. In one study, 72 percent of people agreed that testing cosmetics on animals is wrong.

Another criticism comes from defenders of women's rights. Some of these people question the traditional pressure on women to wear makeup. Others dislike the promotion of glamorous images in magazines and on television. They consider that it creates an unrealistic ideal that causes many young people to worry too much about their appearance.

[13] **critic:** a person who expresses disagreement with something or disapproval of someone

What do you think? Does makeup cause real problems, or is it a harmless part of our social lives? Read these questions and give your opinion.

1. Do you think animal testing for cosmetics is OK, or should it be illegal? Would you buy cosmetics if you knew they had been tested on animals?

2. Is our society too fashion-conscious? How do TV and magazines affect our self-image?

3. Where and when do you think it is OK to wear makeup? Are there any situations where people shouldn't wear makeup?

4. What is the difference in makeup use in your society between women and men? Do you think these differences should exist?

5. Does the amount of cosmetics someone uses affect your opinion of him or her? What do you think of people who don't use cosmetics?

6. What cosmetic products do you use often? Is your use of cosmetics more about taking care of your skin or looking good in a social situation?

Video Quest

Junk Food and Acne

Watch this video to learn about the connection between junk food and acne. What causes acne?

After You Read

Read the sentences and choose Ⓐ, Ⓑ, Ⓒ, or Ⓓ.

1 Which part of the skin forms the defensive layer?
- Ⓐ hypodermis
- Ⓑ dermis
- Ⓒ epidermis
- Ⓓ nerve endings

2 Why do most chameleons change color?
- Ⓐ To hide from predators
- Ⓑ To make themselves invisible
- Ⓒ Because of the temperature
- Ⓓ Because of the landscape

3 Why do people think that the zebra's camouflage works?
- Ⓐ Because their predators can't see the color black.
- Ⓑ Because it confuses their predators.
- Ⓒ Because the stripes help them hide in trees.
- Ⓓ Because the stripes make them look smaller.

4 Why do Samoan men have tattoos?
- Ⓐ To show which tribe they belong to
- Ⓑ To show others that they are brave
- Ⓒ To remember important information
- Ⓓ To try to be more attractive

5 Among which people did tattoos first become highly fashionable in the late 19th century?
- Ⓐ the upper classes of American society
- Ⓑ the upper classes of British society
- Ⓒ sailors
- Ⓓ pop stars

6 What does recent investigation show about opinions of tattoos?

(A) They make people's appearance better.

(B) They make people seem less reliable.

(C) They are seen as unattractive.

(D) They are worn by criminals.

7 Why did pale skin go out of fashion?

(A) Doctors realized sun was important for good health.

(B) More people began to work outside.

(C) Pale makeup took skin off.

(D) Chalk was found to be bad for the skin.

8 What should you do to take care of your skin?

(A) Get more than 20 minutes of sun a day.

(B) Wash pimples as often as possible.

(C) Wear makeup for protection.

(D) Try not to worry about things.

Which Chapter?

Match the information with four chapters from the book.

Which chapter discusses . . .

_____ **1** an explorer?

_____ **2** a negative view of a suntan?

_____ **3** how human skin protects us?

_____ **4** the dangers of beauty products?

_____ **5** camouflage?

_____ **6** a couple finding a frozen mummy?

_____ **7** tribes painting their faces and bodies?

_____ **8** the skin's color created by melanin?

A Chapter 1: Skin

B Chapter 2: The First Line of Defense

C Chapter 3: Body Art

D Chapter 4: Makeup

Answer Key

Words to Know, page 4
1 wrinkles **2** tattoo **3** cosmetics **4** lipstick **5** acne
6 suntan

Words to Know, page 5
1 dye **2** prey **3** organ **4** camouflage **5** predator

Predict, page 5
Answers will vary.

Video Quest, page 10
It has lots of quills that can penetrate the skin of the predator and even kill it.

Analyze, page 15
Traditions spread when people travel.

Video Quest, page 17
Firemen, to help identify their bodies.

Evaluate, page 21
Answers will vary.

Evaluate, page 23
Answers will vary.

Video Quest, page 25
Stress is one cause of acne.

Choose the Correct Answers, page 26
1 C **2** C **3** B **4** B **5** B **6** B **7** A **8** D

Which chapter?, page 27
1 C **2** D **3** A **4** D **5** B **6** C **7** D **8** A